Visiting Day

Dedicated to: Rebecca Kristine & Lillian Elizabeth

by:
Jay Robert Bales

Illustrated by:
Nancy Thomas-Law and Nancy J. Stephens
Content Consultant:
Richard Jackson M.D.

authorHOUSE®

AuthorHouse™
1663 Liberty Drive
Bloomington, IN 47403
www.authorhouse.com
Phone: 1-800-839-8640

First published by AuthorHouse 2/23/2010

ISBN: 978-1-4490-8215-4 (e)
ISBN: 978-1-4490-8214-7 (sc)

Library of Congress Control Number: 2010901954

Printed in the United States of America
Bloomington, Indiana

This book is printed on acid-free paper.

Summary: Discusses, in simple text and illustrations, scenes that began with children discussing how and who is in prison, what programs and activities are available in prison and what happens when a person is first released from prison.

Interior design by Jay R. Bales

Readers Guide

This book is meant to help open a line of communications between the middle school reader and a loved one or family friend who is in prison. It is the authors hope that valuable information will be received by the reader and used as a foundation of learning and understanding more about the Criminal Justice System from the time a person is arrested to the time they are released from prison.

This book is also meant to help the reader understand that they are not the only one who has a loved one or friend of the family in prison. Those who are imprisoned are from every socio-economic level of our communities.

Lastly, it is the hope of the author that the reader realizes they are not responsible for the negative behavior of those who have been sentence to prison. They are however a very important reason why someone in prison should want to return home and never return to prison away from their loved ones.

It was another warm summer morning in the inner city. Brittany Stanley and a younger neighbor girl, Dazia Anderson were setting on Brittany's grandmother's front porch talking and playing with Dazia's kitten. Devan, Dazia's older brother and Corie, Brittany's twin brother had just finished playing baseball and decided to stop and talk before going to Devan's house to play computer games. Corie was wearing his favorite baseball jersey and his catchers mask was propped on top of his head.

Brittany, Corie, Dazia & Devan

About the time Corie and Devan sat down to talk with Brittany and Dazia, grandma Stanley came to the front door and said, "Remember today is visiting day. We will be leaving at noon to visit with your mother." Grandma Stanley said, "Oh I didn't know you had friends over. Good morning children."

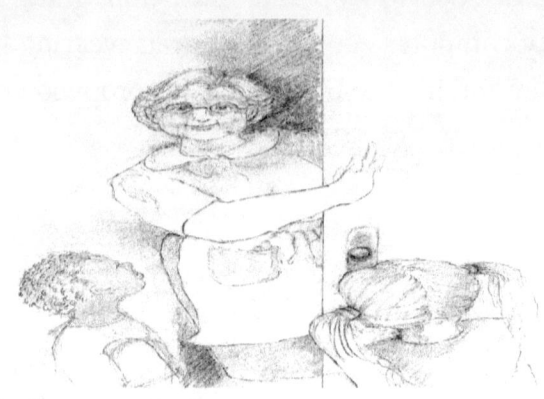

Brittany said, "Grandma I'd like to introduce you to our new neighbors, Devan and Dazia Anderson." Grandma Stanley replied, "Welcome to the neighborhood Devan and Dazia. Devan and Dazia responded, "Thank you very much grandma Stanley."

After grandma Stanley closed the door, Dazia said, "Where do you go to visit your mom, Brittany? Brittany responded, "At prison." Dazia responded, "What is a **prison (pris-on)**?" Devan attempted to stop his little sister from asking too many questions and said, "Stop asking so many questions Dazia."

Corie said, that's O.K. Devan we don't mind answering questions about our mom being in prison. Our mom said, "We have nothing to be ashamed of or embarrassed about. We have done nothing wrong. She is **responsible (re-spon-si-ble)** for her behavior." Corie said, "To answer your question Dazia, our mom said a prison is like a small **community (com-mu-ni-ty)**. She tells us that there are buildings with small rooms that are called cells which are assigned to each prisoner to live in until they go home. There is a school with classrooms, a library, a gymnasium, health care for medical needs, a dentist office, a grocery store, which is called a commissary and food service where everyone eats. Large prisons sometimes have a church for worship."

Corie continued, "All of the buildings are surrounded by high fences with alarms. They have sharp coiled wire on the top of the fence, and at the bottom to help prevent anyone from escaping. Our mom also said that some prisons even have towers where corrections officers are assigned. The towers are high enough to see for long distances to better watch prisoners as they go to and from activities, such as school, work, to eat or anytime they come close to the fence for any reason."

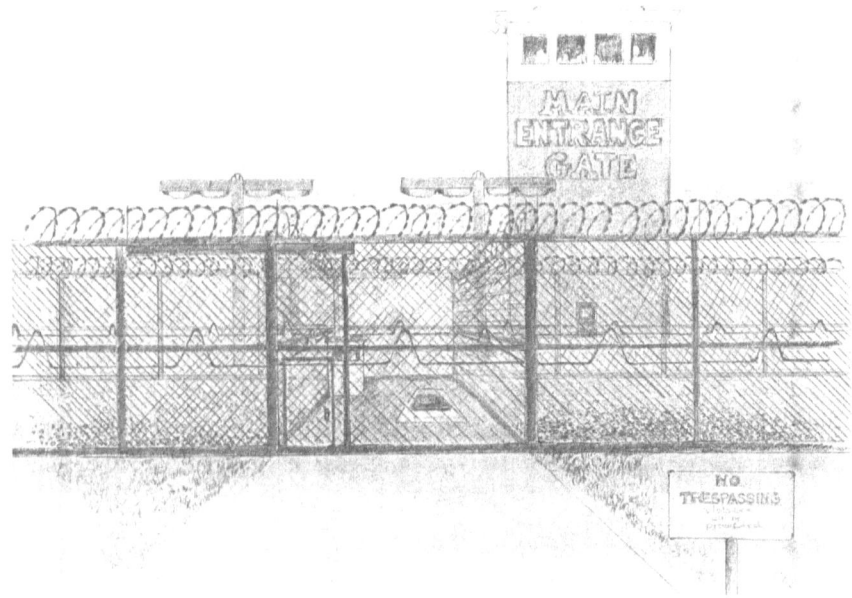

"At night, our mom said that the prison is lit up, almost like daytime, with hundreds of lights mounted on high poles and the sides of buildings. This is to better able the correction staff to see at night, almost as well as they can see in the daylight."

Dazia asked Brittany, "Well, who is in prison?"

Brittany said, "Our mom said that grandfathers, grandmothers, fathers, mothers, brothers, sisters, uncles, aunts, cousins and friends.

Our mom said that anyone who has committed a serious crime, called a **felony (felo-ny)** and is **convicted (con-victed)** of the felony, can be **sentenced (sen-tenced)** by a judge to spend one year or more in prison."

When you hear that a person is locked up in jail because they are believed to have committed a crime, that is much different. Sometimes before the person is scheduled to stand trial they must spend time in jail, for the safety of others, or to make sure they will show up for their **trial (tri-al).**

There are also some crimes called **misdemeanors (mis-de-menors)** that are believed to be less severe because they do not cause as much harm to others. A person who is found to be responsible for committing a misdemeanor is said to be guilty and is also sentenced by a judge to spend less than one year in a city or county jail.

"Brittany, you said something about a court and a judge. What is a court, and what does a judge do?" asked Dazia.

Brittany quickly responded to Dazia's question, "Our mom said that court is a place where a person who has been **arrested (ar-rested)** is scheduled to go and explain what happened. Sometimes people explain to a judge and jury, or sometimes only to a judge. They explain why they should not have been arrested, by telling what happened according to them. Sometimes the arrested person will admit to committing a crime, or explain why they should not be found responsible for the crime, or should not receive the maximum punishment for their involvement in a crime."

The judge, who is sometimes called a **magistrate (mag-is-trate)** or **("your honor")** is the person who makes sure that the arrested person has the **opportunity (op-por-tu-ni-ty)** to explain his or her involvement in a crime. The judge is also responsible for making sure everyone in the courtroom understands the law which is believed to have been **violated (vi-o-lated),** and the role of each person involved who must prove or disprove whether the law was violated by the arrested person.

The judge makes decisions during the trial about the fairness of the facts presented at the trial by the **prosecutor (pros-e-cutor)** and the defense attorney. The prosecutor represents the citizens. The **defense (de-fense)** attorney represents the **defendant (de-fen dant)** or accused.

At the end of the trial, the judge decides the appropriate amount of punishment the defendant should receive, if it is proven that he or she was responsible for violating the law.

Dazia said, "Now I understand what a judge is responsible for, but what is a jury? What are they responsible for?"

Corie responded, "Our mom said that a jury might have 10, or even more adults who are asked to make the final decision of guilt or innocence. The number of jurors vary because extra are selected to hear the evidence in case one **juror (jur-or)** gets ill or can not complete serving for any other reason. The extra juror will be ready to replace them.

A juror may have a job such as a school teacher, janitor, banker, secretary, plumber, waitress, business owner, nurse and even a retired person like our grandmother. Jury members are adults who often have jobs and families just like the defendant."

A juror is responsible for listening to the facts that are presented by the prosecuting attorney, the defense attorney, the defendant and any victim or witness in the case. A victim or witness may be asked to explain facts which may prove or disprove if the defendant was guilty or not guilty of committing the crime.

After listening to the facts presented a jury is asked to decide whether the defendant is guilty or not guilty of violating the law. Sometimes the defendant decides not to have a jury. Instead they will choose to have only the judge, or magistrate, decide their guilt or innocence. This is sometimes called a "bench trial" because the judge, who is seated at a bench type structure, decides guilt or innocence.

Then Dazia said, "Now I understand who may be sentenced to jail and prison and what happens in court, but what happens next?" Devan said, "Dazia, that is enough questions. Brittany and Corie may not want to talk about their mom being in prison."

Brittany responded, "That's O.K. Devin, we don't mind that's how you learn new things, buy asking a lot of questions. Our mom said that the judge explained to her that because she had been found guilty of committing a serious crime she would be sentence to prison. The judge then briefly explained to our mom her right to challenge anything that happened at the trial that she believed was not fairly or properly presented. In so doing, sometimes a person may be released from prison because they were not given a fair opportunity to prove their innocence or may receive a new trial that could turn out better for them. This is known as the appeal process. Many times appeals are not accepted by the Court of Appeals because the trial court made no errors.

Brittany continued, "Our mom said after the judge explained her right to appeal she was immediately taken from the courtroom to jail. After staying a few days in jail our mom was driven by police officers to the nearest female correctional facility. Once the police dropped her off at the prison our mom was fingerprinted, assigned a number and had her photograph taken. A copy of the photograph was added to other papers that was brought from the sentencing court. Another copy of the photograph was used to make her an identification badge, much like a driver's license or the kind some schools have for each student. The number that was assigned to our mom is printed on her identification badge and on all her prison clothing and personal property.

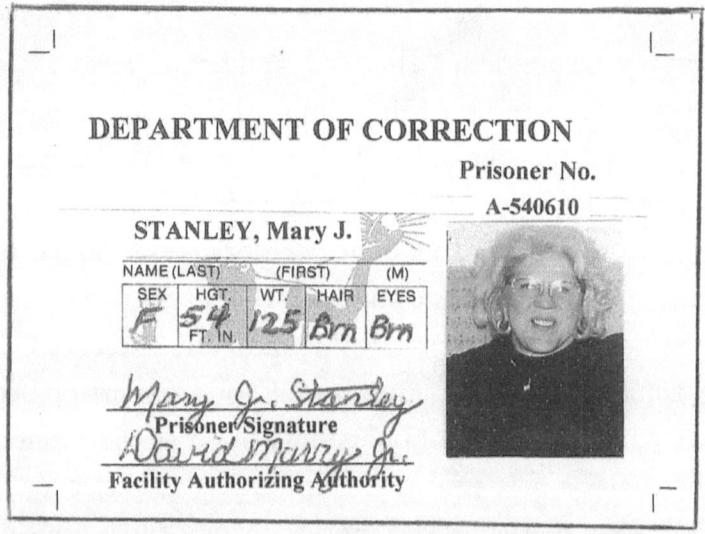

Our mom said a file folder was made up and all the information that was brought by the police and that prepared by the correction staff was placed in the file folder. On the outside of the file folder is her name, prison number, crime found guilty of and the dates representing the minimum and maximum amount of time she will spend in prison. This folder is kept by correction staff to record any activities our mom is involved in while in prison, whether good or bad, such as school, work assignments, religious activities or misconduct reports for violating rules."

Devan said, "What happened next? Brittany said, "Our mom told us that in the first few days she was given additional clothing and assigned to a room, which is also called a cell. The correction staff scheduled and taught lessons daily about what services and activities are available to prisoners and the expected behavior of a prisoner who wants to stay out of trouble while in prison."

Devan, "So each prisoner has their own room?" Corie responded, "No, our mom tells us that not all prisons have cells for each prisoner. At some prisons cells are shared with other prisoners and some prisoners live in large open rooms called dormitories that have many prisoner living together."

Corie then said, "After our mom was assigned where she would live until moved, transferred or released she was examined by a medical doctor to see whether she had any physical problems that required immediate treatment or that might require a follow up appointment. She then was seen by a dentist who examined her teeth and determine what follow up dental care might be necessary.

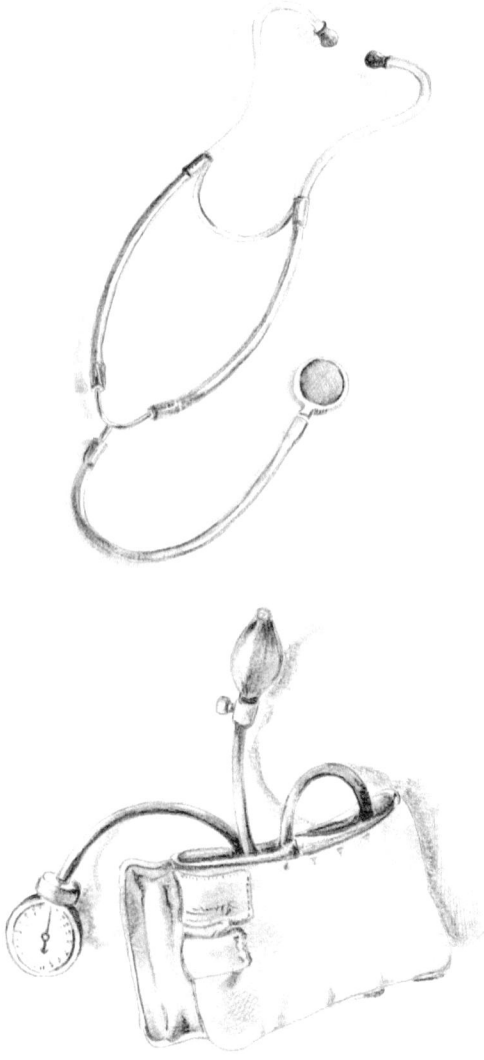

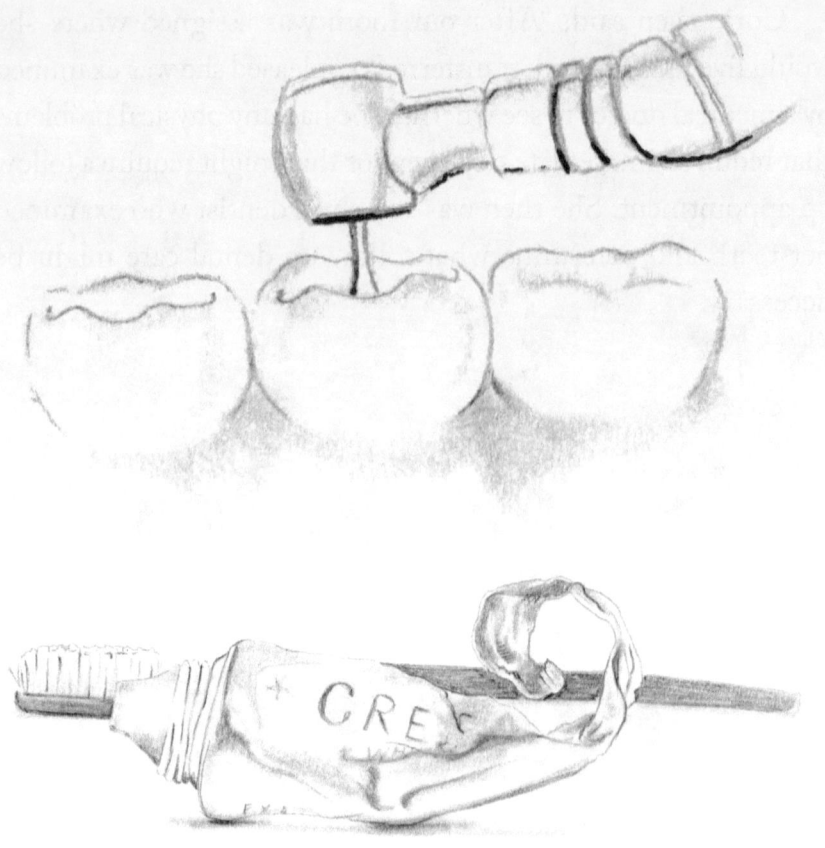

Brittany said, "Our mom told us that during her first several weeks in prison she was not allowed to have a visit or go to activities with prisoners who were not in **quarantine (quar-an-tine),** which means to be kept separate from others. New prisoners are kept in quarantine to make sure they do not have an illnesses that another might catch. This is also a good time for correction staff to closely look at the prisoners file folder and determine where in the prison system the prisoner should be transferred.

Brittany continued, "Our mom said she also had to take several written tests. Just like we do in school: Math, English,

Reading and History. The test are used to see whether a prisoner must attend school and at what grade level they should begin learning. Our mom said not all prisoners must go to school but many often do."

Dazia, "Does your mother live in a cell now? Brittany, "No, she now lives in a dormitory. When our mom first arrived at prison she lived in a cell with another **inmate (in-mate)**,which is a different name for prisoner. Each time we wrote our mother a letter we needed to address the envelop with the prison name, address, our mothers name, prison number, cell number and bed in the cell. In prison the numbers are used to help staff locate a prisoner very quickly.

Each cell number is painted on the cell door, door frame or near the cell door much like a house address. Our mom said the rooms are smaller than our bedrooms at home. Many times two prisoners share a cell so there is very little room for personal property. Some prisons permit prisoners to have a television set, radio and some personal clothing.

To discourage prisoners not to steal from each other and prevent one prisoner from having more expensive personal property than another the furnishing are provided and personal property can not cost more than allowed by the prison. Each cell is equipped with the same type of bed, table, chair and locker. Having a small amount of property and the same furnishings helps make it easier for correction officers to inspect the cell for cleanliness and **contraband (con-tra-band)**, which is property that a prisoner is not allowed to posses such as extra clothing , stolen property, altered property, drugs or a weapon."

Devan said, "Now I better understand why prisoners are assigned to cells and why the cell number is important when you write, but why is each prison inmate assigned a number?"

Brittany, Corie, Dazia & Devan

Corey responded, our mom said a prison number is assigned basically to help correction staff to keep track of each prisoner. Something like a student identification number that is assigned to only one student at a school and is included on their identification card.

A prison number is used to track a prisoner anywhere in a prison system, no matter how large the prison system may be.

Our mom said the correction staff often call her by last name and prison number. By adding the prisoner number the staff eliminate another prisoner having the same last name thinking the corrections staff wants them. Each time a prisoners last name and number is called those prisoners having the same last name as others listen close for the number to see if they are being called by staff.

Each time correction staff must count prisoners they must show their identification badge and say their prison number if asked. This helps correction staff to assure that the right prisoner is being counted. Corrections staff must take count at designated times during each work shift to make sure all prisoners are where they should be or have not escaped. Correction staff take count much like our school teachers take attendance except more often and even when prisoners are asleep at night and early in the morning." Dazia, "Who was the person you said counted the prisoners?"

Brittany, "Our mom said many correction staff are responsible to ensure prison inmates are where they are suppose to be at all times. Teachers, librarians, maintenance staff, food service staff, counselors and others often count prison inmates by checking their photo identification badge, passes or assignment to validate they belong where they are being counted. The person who is primarily responsible is a correction officer."

Dazia, "Does the Correction Officer do anything else?" Brittany, "Our mom said correction officers supervise the clean up of the living areas, answer questions about the prison activities or make various announcements about activities several prisoners may want to attend or must attend. The correction officer primary responsibility is to ensure the prisoner and staff are safe and that the prisoners are where they are suppose to be at all times.

Brittany, Corie, Dazia & Devan

Sometimes the correction officer is called the police by prisoners because they also enforce the prison rules. A correction officer can write a prisoner a ticket for misconduct when they violate the rules. Just like a police officer can write a citizen a ticket if they violate the law. If a prisoner receives a misconduct ticket and they are found to be guilty they will receive punishment such as; the taking away of privileges, like watching T.V., going to recreation or they may have to work on projects without being paid or the most severe punishment remain longer in prison.

Dazia, "Brittany, you said that even a counselor may be responsible for keeping track of prisoners. What is a counselor and what do they do?" Brittany, "our mom has talked about substance abuse counselors. They are sometimes volunteers and sometime correction staff. They are people who are knowledgeable about substance abuse and what negative behavior drugs can cause. Some prisoners must attend and complete a substance abuse class before they can be released from prison because they were using drugs or alcohol at the time they committed a crime. Some prisoners may attend because they want to learn more about drug and alcohol abuse. Our mom attends because she wants to learn more and maybe someday teach classes about substance abuse and how it effects the drug or alcohol user and those around them.

Corie, "Our mom has talked about a counselor who is responsible to ensure that daily the building she lives in is clean, safe and secure. Sometimes they are called housing unit counselors, managers or supervisors. They are also responsible for the safe keeping of each prisoner file folders that live in their housing unit. The counselor is responsible for recording accomplishments and sometimes negative conduct in the prisoner files. Much like our teachers keep grades and notes about students in their classroom.

A counselor has days and times scheduled when a prisoner can sit down and talk with them. Often times the prisoner is seen by a counselor to receive some assistance with a problem or concern that they may have, such as, what prison activities might be best for them to improve, seek employment when released or to change their job in the prison. Dazia, "Is the counselor in charge of the whole prison?"

Brittany, "No, our mother said a Warden is in charge of the prison. She said the Warden is like a chief of police or a principal of a school. A Warden is responsible for everything that happens to a prisoner while they are in the prison they manage.

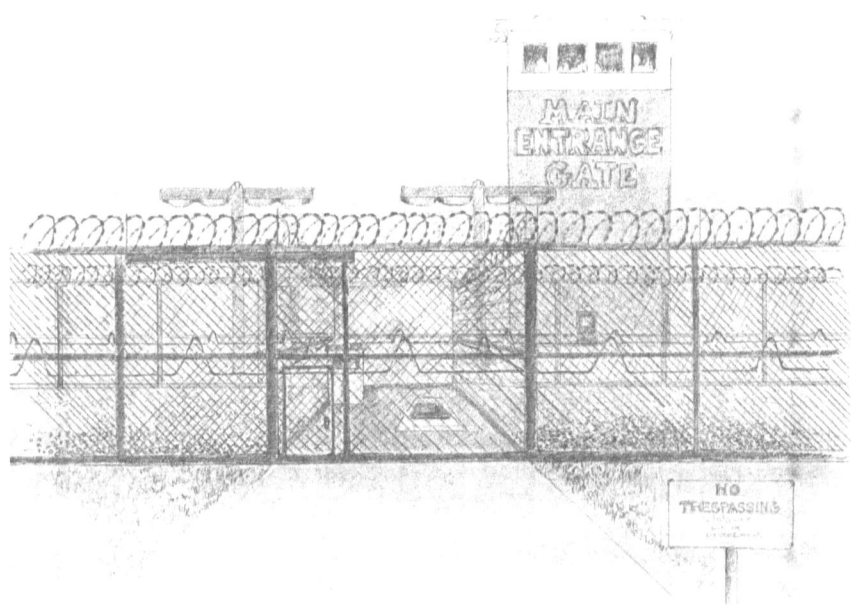

The Warden makes sure that corrections staff treat the prisoners humanely and respectfully. The Warden has many people who work for them, such as; medical doctor, nurses, dentist, dental hygienist, psychologist, counselors, school teachers, food service staff, librarian, maintenance worker, correction officer supervisors, corrections officers and others.

The Warden is also responsible for what programs are available to the prisoners such as academic (school), vocational programs where job skills are learned, recreation, the library, religious services, substance abuse treatment, visiting and other programs. All of these activities cost money and the staff and prisoners who work at the prison must also be paid which is another responsibility of the Warden.

The Warden also meets with prisoners who represent large numbers of other prisoners to discuss what improvements can be made to programs or how everything is going in the prisoner living and work areas. The Warden also holds meetings with staff about what improvements are needed and what is going well at the prison. The meetings with the prisoners and the staff help the Warden to better understand what daily activities are running smoothly and which ones may need more attention to improve. Dazia, "Brittany, you said the Warden meets with the prisoners and staff to discuss programs. What programs would a prisoner talk about?

Brittany, "Our mom represents the prisoners that live in the same housing unit as she does and sometimes they ask her to talk about whether a new program can be added to the ones already offered. My mom goes to school to learn how to use computers. Others go to school because they must complete their high school education. Some prisoners who already have a high school education would like to learn the skills to become a plumber, electrician or carpenter assistant for example.

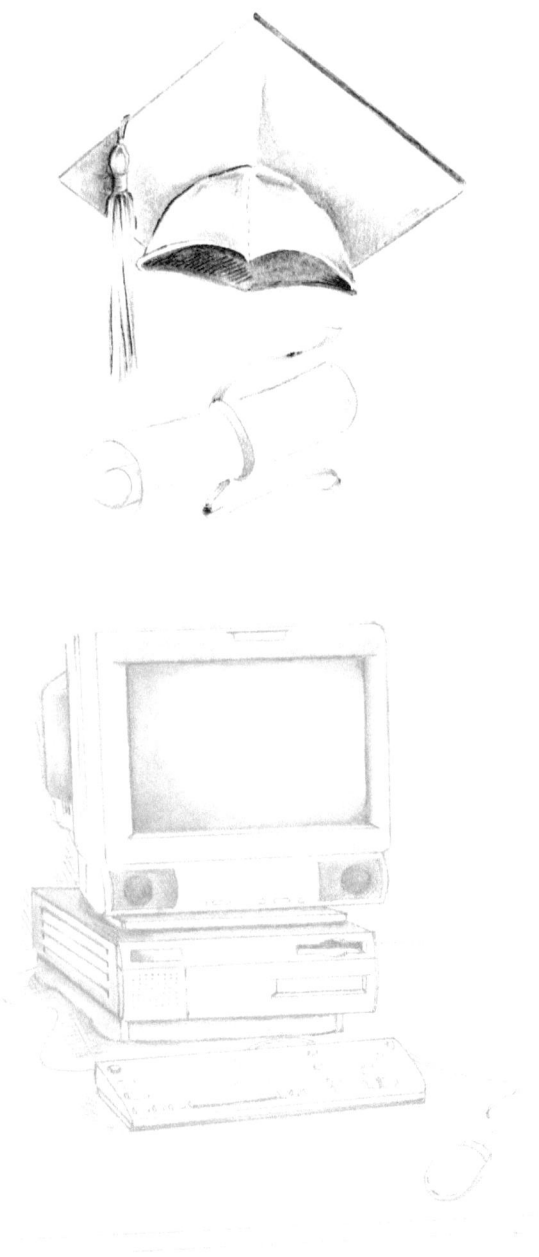

Our mom said that the most important programs are related to earning a high school education. All other programs offered are usually related to learning a job skill. Not every new program recommended by the prisoners are considered or made available because of the cost to the prison. Some new programs are considered if they are provided at very little cost. Often times these programs are the responsibility of volunteers who provide the instruction and sometimes the necessary materials.

Our mom said that if a new program is recommended that would help prisoners to become employable and the cost of it can be proven to be worth while by the prison staff then the program may be tried as a pilot or test program to see if it will be of benefit. So the prisoners never give up trying to get new programs."

Devan, "Can a prisoner work and earn money while in prison?

Brittany, Corie, Dazia & Devan

Corie, "Yes, our mom once worked in the prisoner store helping bag prisoner store purchases such as food, hygiene products or snacks. Our mom would assist the civilian store worker to deliver some prisoners orders to their housing units while other prisoners would be scheduled to pick up their purchases at the prisoner store. Our mom said that the prisoner store worker job did not pay as well as others so she signed up for other job assignments that would pay even better and help her obtain employment once paroled from prison.

Devan responded, I thought parole was when you were released from jail? Corie replied, no Devan parole can be given after a prisoner has spent time in prison. A parole is given when a prisoner has spent the amount of time ordered by the trial judge and is believed to be ready to go home because they have shown good behavior while in prison and can be trusted to continue to behave well. Devan, you may be thinking of probation which is a sentence given to a convicted person by the judge and the person is not sent to a jail or prison unless they do not follow the rules of conduct outlined by the judge.

Corie continued, our mom said parole also has conditions that must be met or the person will be returned back to prison. Our mom said the difference between the term parole and probation is often times mixed up by many. Our mom is being accepted into a new program called the prisoner re-entry initiative program. This program is to better prepare prisoners for parole. The re-entry program will help our mom learn new skills for obtaining a job, help her to find affordable housing and introduce her to community support groups that will also help her to stay out of prison. Our mom is very excited about the program and thankful that she will have additional support once out of prison.

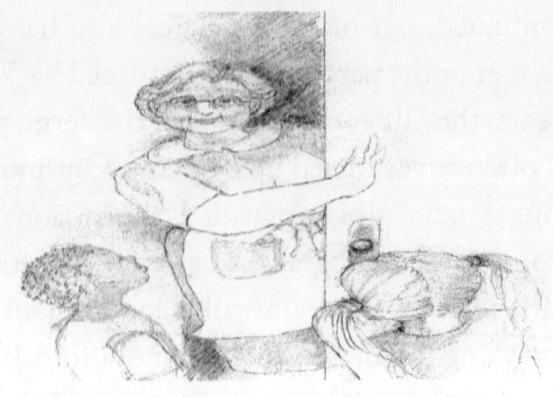

Grandma Stanley opened the door and said, it is time to get ready for our visit. Say goodbye to your new friends Devan and Dazia. Corie and Brittany turned to their new friends and said their goodbyes and assured Devan and Dazia that they would see them again soon.

Glossary

Arrested: ar-rest-ed, -to take to jail or court by authority of the law: *The police arrested the burglar.*

Community: com-mu-ni-ty, -all the people living in the same place: the people of any district or town: *This lake provides water for six communities.*

Contraband: con-tra-band, -goods that the law forbids to be sold or bought or imported or exported. *The visitor was caught smuggling contraband jewelry into the prison.*

Convicted: con-vict-ed, -to prove or declare guilty: *The jury convicted the defendant of theft.*

Convict: con-vict, -a person serving a prison sentence for some crime. *Some people refer to a prisoner or inmate as a convict.*

Custody: cus-to-dy, -in jail, prison or the care of the police: *The person accused of the robbery is now in police custody.*

Defendant: de-fen-dant, -one who is, kept safe;, guarded from attack or harm;, or protect:, or *Lawyers are hired to defend people known as defendants; these are people who have been charged with crimes.*

Defense: de-fense, -any thing or act that defends, guards, or protects: *The defendant's attorney presented a strong defense with evidence to support that he was at home when the crime was committed.*

Felony: fel-o-ny, -a major crime, such as murder, arson, or robbery, for which the law provides greater punishment than for a misdemeanor: *The police arrested the arsonist within hours of setting a building on fire, which is a felony.*

Inmate: in-mate, -a person kept in a prison: *Inmate Stanley is assigned to a work detail in the prison law library.*

Juror: jur-or, -a member of a jury.

Jury: jur-y, -a group of citizens selected to hear evidence in a case brought before a court of law: *Based on the evidence presented during the trial, the jury found the defendant guilty of committing burglary.*

Magistrate: *mag-is-trate,* -an officer of the government who has power to apply the law and put it in force: *The magistrate ordered the convicted man to serve two years in prison.*

Misdemeanor: mis-de-mean-or, -any minor breaking of the law or of a municipal ordinance, for which the punishment is less than for a felony: *The man was arrested for destruction of property and charged with a misdemeanor because the value of the property was less than is required for a felony.*

Opportunity: *op-por-tu-ni-ty,* -a good chance; favorable time: *I have had no opportunity to telephone my best friend, Corie, this weekend.*

Prison: pris-on, -a public building in which criminals are confined: *The convicted killer was sentenced to life in prison without the possibility of parole.*

Prosecutor: pros-e-cu-tor, -the prosecutor decides what crimes an arrested person will be charged with in a court of law: *The prosecutor represented the victim of the armed robbery.*

Quarantine: quar-an-tine, -to keep a person, animal, plant, or ship away from others for a time to prevent the spread of an infectious disease: *The prisoners were in quarantine for thirty days to make sure they did not have a disease that could be spread in the prison system.*

Responsible: re-spon-si-ble, -having the duty or obligation of taking care of someone or something: *The correction officer is responsible for knowing where the prisoners assigned to his or her housing unit at all times.*

Trial: tri-al, -the examining of evidence and deciding of a case in court: *The accused was brought to trial.*

Violate: vi-o-late, -to break a rule, law, promise, or agreement, or to defy instructions: *Driving through a red light is a violation of traffic laws.*

About Author, Content Consultant & Illustrators

Jay R. Bales is a retired Deputy Prison Warden 3 with over twenty years' tenure. Jay was a licensed private investigator for more than fifteen years and has over twenty-five years' experience with physical security, investigation, and handwriting analysis. His academic degrees include a B. A. in Organizational Development and a M. A. in Organizational Management from Spring Arbor University in Spring Arbor Michigan. He is an Adjunct Instructor for a Michigan University, teaching in the Criminal Justice curriculum. This is the first book Jay has written.

Nancy Thomas Law received her BFA from Miami University of Ohio, with a degree in drawing and painting and additional requirements met for teaching certification in Art. She has taught high school art in the public schools of Pennsylvania as well as participated in numerous local and regional juried art shows. She is a former member of the Board of Directors of the North Hills Art Center in Pittsburgh, Pa. The mother of two and grandmother of one. Nancy currently resides in Pittsburgh with her husband. An upcoming move back to her hometown of Chagrin Falls, Ohio will bring things full circle and return her to her roots.

Nancy J. Stephens is a self taught artist of ten years and has exhibited her works in local juried annual art shows. This is Nancy's first contribution of illustrations to a reading text.

Richard Jackson M.D. is a Diplomate of the American Board of Psychiatry and Neurology Adult, Adolescent, and Child Psychiatry with Certification in the Subspecialty of Forensic Psychiatry. Doctor Jackson is an Associate Clinical Professor of Psychiatry at the Wayne State University School of Medicine Department of Psychiatry. Doctor Jackson is also an Assistant Clinical Adjunct Professor of Psychiatry at University of Michigan School of Medicine Department of Psychiatry.